EVERYTHING ABOUT *ME*

A Guide for My Future Caregivers

Families of Children with Special Needs Edition

Dee Marrella
With Dennis McClellan

PRESS LLC

SANFORD • FLORIDA

EVERYTHING ABOUT *ME*
--- 👬 ---

Copyright © 2011 by Dee Marrella, All rights reserved.

Published by DC Press, 2445 River Tree Circle, Sanford, FL 32771
www.focusonethics.com or www.dcpressbooks.com

No part of this publication may be reproduced, stored in a retrieval system, or transmitted in any form or by any means, electronic, mechanical, photocopying, recording, scanning, or otherwise, except as permitted under Section 107 or 108 of the 1976 United States Copyright Act, without either the prior written permission of the Publisher, or authorization through payment of the per-copy fee to the Copyright Clearance Center, In., 222 Rosewood Drive, Danvers, MA 01923, (978) 750-8400, fax (978) 646-8600, or on the web at www.copyright.com. Request to the Publisher for permission should be addressed to the Permissions Department, DC Press, 2445 River Tree Circle, Sanford, FL 32771, (407) 688-1156,fax (407) 688-1135, or contacting the Publisher at info@focusonethics.com or info@dcpressbooks.com

Limit of Liability/Disclaimer of Warranty: While the Publisher and Author have used their best efforts in preparing this book, they make no representations or warranties with respect to the accuracy or completeness of the contents of this book and specifically disclaim any implied warranties of merchantability or fitness for a particular purpose. No warranty may be created or extended by sales representatives or written sales materials. The advice and strategies contained herein may not be suitable for your situation. The publisher is not engaged in rendering professional services, and you should consult with a professional (such as an attorney, physician, financial advisor) where appropriate. Neither the Publisher nor Author shall be liable for any loss of profit or other commercial damages, including but not limited to special, incidental, consequential, or other damages.

For general information on our other products and services please contact our offices at 407-688-1156 and/or go to www.focusonethics.com or www.dcpress.com.

This book was set in Times New Roman and Arial
Cover Design and Composition by Debra Deysher

Everything About Me, Families of Children With Special Needs Edition
ISBN: 978-1-932021-57-8

First DC Press Edition
Printed in the United States of America
10 9 8 7 6 5 4 3 2 1

EVERYTHING ABOUT *ME*

I dedicate this book to those who have found room in their hearts to sacrifice and give an abundance of love to a child in special need. These children are the "innocents."

The following story is only one small example of a challenged child's love and compassion.

Who Won?

I saw a beautiful example of kindness during the Special Olympics track and field meet. One participant was Kim Peek, a brain-damaged severely handicapped boy racing in the 50-yard dash.

Kim was racing against two other athletes with cerebral palsy. They were in wheelchairs, Kim was the lone runner. As the gun sounded, Kim moved quickly ahead of the other two. Twenty yards ahead and 10 yards from the finish line, he turned to see how the others were coming. The girl had turned her wheelchair around and was stuck against the wall. The other boy was pushing his wheelchair backward with his feet. Kim stopped, went back and pushed the little girl across the finish line. The boy in the wheelchair going backward won the race. The girl took second. Kim lost.

Or did he? The crowd gave Kim a standing ovation.

- Dan Clark
From Chicken Soup for the Woman's Soul
Text © 1996 Dan Clark
Health Communications, Inc,

EVERYTHING ABOUT *ME*

A NOTE TO MY CAREGIVERS

The information in this book is directed specifically to those people family, close friends, and the strangers who might one day serve as my caregivers. Those days may not come for many months or years. However, when you read the words on these pages, my family / guardian and I have done our very best to help you "get to know me" "who I am, when these words were written down" – so you might "understand me." There has also been an attempt to "understand you" – my caregivers, and the highly important role you will play in my life in the future.

Thanks in advance.

EVERYTHING ABOUT *ME*

CONTENTS

v
— For My Caregivers —

xiii
— Why You Need To Complete This Book —

xv
— How to Complete this Book —

xix
— General Guidance for My Caregivers —

xxi
— A Note from my Parents / Guardians —

PART I: MY FAMILY	**1**
Personal Information	2
Parent / Guardian Information	4
Siblings	5
Grandparents' Information	9
Chart of Descendents	10
Close Relatives Information	11

EVERYTHING ABOUT *ME*

PART II: ABOUT ME — 15

My Profile	17
My Favorite Product Brands	19
My Personality	23
My Typical Day	26
My Favorite Foods	29
Food Restrictions	30
Food Facts and Me	31
My Physical Capabilities	35
Entertainment Preferences	42
Caring for My Pets	44
Additional Information About Me	53
My Education	59
Employment	64

PART III: MEDICAL — 67

Important To Know About Me Medically	69
Immunization Information	77
Drug and Medical Allergies	78
Medical Healthcare Support Team	79
Programs Regularly Participated In	83
Family Medical History	85

EVERYTHING ABOUT *ME*

PART IV: FINANCES — 89

Income Sources	90
Details of Monthly Expenses	91

PART V: MY NON-MEDICAL TEAM — 97

Professional Services	99
Insurance Policies	101
My Family Social Support Team	108
Local, State and Federal Government Assistance	109
Advocacy Support Team	111

PART VI: MY FUTURE CARE — 115

Caregiving	116
If and When I Face a Terminal Situation	117
Organ Donation	119

PART VII: FAITH & RELIGION IN MY LIFE — 123

Religious Affiliation	124
Reflections on My Life Thus Far	126
A Letter to My Loved Ones	128

EVERYTHING ABOUT *ME*

PART VIII: HOLIDAYS AND TRADITIONS — 131

Holidays & Traditions — 132

Family History & Memories — 135

PART IX: MEMORIAL PREFERENCES — 141

Preferred Funeral Home And Burial Location — 142

Clothing And Mementos — 143

Place Of Worship — 143

Pallbearers — 144

Floral Tributes / Donations — 145

Obituary Information — 146

NOTES — 147

AUTHOR'S COMMENTS — 169

ABOUT DEE MARRELLA — 171

ABOUT DENNIS McCLELLAN — 172

PUBLISHER'S COMMENTS — 173

EMERGENCY WALLET CARD — 179

> "THE CENTRAL STRUGGLE OF PARENTHOOD IS TO LET OUR HOPES FOR OUR CHILDREN OUTWEIGH OUR FEARS."
>
> *~Ellen Goodman~*

WHY THIS BOOK IS IMPORTANT & WHY IT SHOULD BE COMPLETED SOONER THAN LATER

In speaking with parents and guardians of children with special needs, one of the ever-present concerns is the question of what happens to the caregiving needs of the child, if "we" (parents/guardians) die or become incapacitated before the child. This is a highly important point that this book can help mitigate.

More than a book, this is a "TOOL" a true tool that you can count on in the event that one day you find your child with special needs in the hands of a caregiver other than yourselves. All important information about me is organized and centralized. This book goes beyond writing a "Letter of Intent."

Every aspect of the life of your child has been taken into consideration and will be found on these pages. If additional information is required, please use the "NOTES" section at the back of the book

Fill out only those questions, sections and pages that apply to your situation and are meaningful to you. The reason for making this book as comprehensive as possible is simple: you want to have a voice in the future caregiving of your loved one.

You can always update things, as needed, at any time.

* This guide is also available in electronic format, that can be completed, printed, saved, and shared.

EVERYTHING ABOUT *ME*

HOW TO COMPLETE THIS BOOK

When filling in spaces and answering questions on the following pages, keep in mind that you are preparing a true "gift" for your family and loved ones as well as those people in the future (possibly strangers) who may be the caregivers for your special child.

Having a voice in one's own caregiving is important to all of us. It is even more important to have the "voice" of special children heard regardless of how that voice gets heard and respected.

As we often point out, this book is a form of "love insurance." By completing the pages, you will be making people in the future (even family members) more aware of who this special child really is and what they want, desire, and need to be done to provide them with the best possible life and care.

By not putting off the job of tackling these pages, you will be giving your child (regardless of their age) a foot up on receiving better caregiving. By talking with family and friends, letting them know that you are preparing this book, will allow those who love your child to participate in completing the information.

And when completed, let people know the book exists. Tell your attorney, doctors, other healthcare providers, clergy, and family members. Perhaps you'll want to complete multiple copies and make sure these important people have a copy close for use when necessary.

REMEMBER: This is a living document. It is a work in progress. It never stops expanding and becoming more exact. It truly is "love insurance."

"SOME PEOPLE COME INTO OUR LIVES, LEAVE FOOTPRINTS ON OUR HEARTS, AND WE ARE NEVER THE SAME."

~ Franz Peter Schubert ~

EVERYTHING ABOUT *ME*

GENERAL GUIDANCE FOR MY CAREGIVERS

I pray that if I need care:

- I will be kept clean.

- I will be fed nutritious meals.

- I will be helped to keep my dignity as much as possible.

- I will obtain necessary medical care.

- I will not be treated as though I am already dead.

- I hope I will have the opportunity to continue to be around things I love – family, friends, jokes, music, movies, and good food until the day I do die!!

- I hope to be remembered for the love and support I tried to give to my family and friends. To be loved in return is to have true wealth.

While I am in a "rational" state, I do realize that if I am injured or ill:

- You cannot be with me 24 hours a day.

- You must go on with your life.

- You love me and will try to do your best to help keep me comfortable.

EVERYTHING ABOUT *ME*

- At times, you will feel anger and guilt when I thrash out in frustration. I am not angry with you. I am angry and frustrated that I have become helpless and in need of assistance.

- You did not cause my illness or injury.

- You must also take care of the family and yourself.

Signed: _____

(Signed by Person with Special Needs if Possible)

EVERYTHING ABOUT *ME*

A Loving Message from My Parents / Guardians to those who might care for me in the future:

> **"TO THE WORLD YOU MAY BE ONE PERSON, BUT TO ONE PERSON YOU MAY BE THE WORLD."**
>
> *~ Heather Cortez ~*

MY FAMILY

PART I

MY FAMILY

The first section of this book contains personal information about my family and ME. Here you will learn about each family member and their involvement in my life.

EVERYTHING ABOUT *ME*

PERSONAL INFORMATION

Last Name: _____

First Name: _____

Nickname: _____

Named After: _____

Birth Date: _____

Place of Birth: _____

Social Security # or Where Located: _____

Location of BIRTH CERTIFICATE: _____

Two People who have certified copies of my birth

Name: _____

Address: _____

Phone: _____

Email: _____

Name: _____

Address: _____

Phone: _____

Email: _____

MY FAMILY

My most current address:

_____

_____

Current Phone: _____

Cell: _____

Parent / Guardian's Email: _____

Name of people with whom I currently live:

_____

_____

EVERYTHING ABOUT *ME*

PARENT / GUARDIAN INFORMATION

Father's Full Name: _____

Current Address: _____

Birth Date: _____

Social Security # or Where Located: _____

Home Phone: _____

Work Phone: _____

Occupation: _____

Email Address: _____

Mother's Full Name: _____

Current Address: _____

Birth Date: _____

Social Security # or Where Located: _____

Home Phone: _____

Work Phone: _____

Occupation: _____

Email Address: _____

Notes of Importance: _____
_____

Sibling I relate to the most: _____

MY FAMILY

SIBLING'S PROFILE - Sibling #1

Name of Child : _____

Date of Birth: _____

Place of Birth: _____

Nickname: _____

Has Special Needs Themselves: _____

Not Living With Special Needs (Explain in Detail): _____

_____

_____

Living At Home: _____

Living Elsewhere: _____

Address: _____

Current Phone: _____

Cell Phone: _____

Notes of Importance: _____

_____

_____

EVERYTHING ABOUT *ME*

SIBLING'S PROFILE - Sibling #2

Name of Child : _____

Date of Birth: _____

Place of Birth: _____

Nickname: _____

Has Special Needs Themselves: _____

Not Living With Special Needs (Explain in Detail): _____

_____

_____

Living At Home: _____

Living Elsewhere: _____

Address: _____

Current Phone: _____

Cell Phone: _____

Notes of Importance: _____

_____

_____

MY FAMILY

SIBLING'S PROFILE - Sibling #3

Name of Child : _____

Date of Birth: _____

Place of Birth: _____

Nickname: _____

Has Special Needs Themselves: _____

Not Living With Special Needs (Explain in Detail): _____

_____

_____

Living At Home: _____

Living Elsewhere: _____

Address: _____

Current Phone: _____

Cell Phone: _____

Notes of Importance: _____

_____

_____

EVERYTHING ABOUT *ME*

SIBLING'S PROFILE - Sibling #4

Name of Child : _____

Date of Birth: _____

Place of Birth: _____

Nickname: _____

Has Special Needs Themselves: _____

Not Living With Special Needs (Explain in Detail): _____

_____

_____

Living At Home: _____

Living Elsewhere: _____

Address: _____

Current Phone: _____

Cell Phone: _____

Notes of Importance: _____

_____

_____

MY FAMILY

MY GRANDPARENTS

MATERNAL - My Mother's Family:

Grandmother:
   Name: _____
   Current Address: _____
   _____

   Current Phone #: _____ Cell: _____
   Email/Web Site: _____

Grandfather:
   Name: _____
   Current Address: _____
   _____

   Current Phone #: _____ Cell: _____
   Email/Web Site: _____

PATERNAL - My Father's Family:

Grandmother:
   Name: _____
   Current Address: _____
   _____

   Current Phone #: _____ Cell: _____
   Email/Web Site: _____

Grandfather:
   Name: _____
   Current Address: _____
   _____

   Current Phone #: _____ Cell: _____
   Email/Web Site: _____

*If living

EVERYTHING ABOUT *ME*

My Chart of Descendants

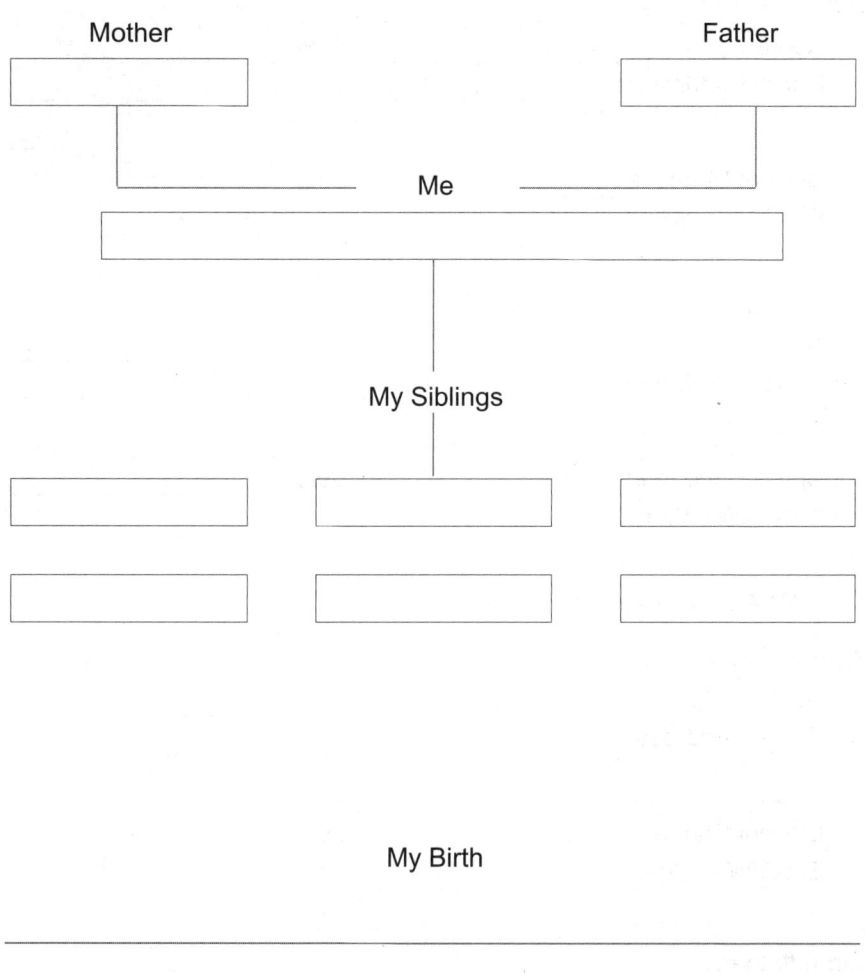

My Birth

MY FAMILY

CLOSE RELATIVES
(Aunts, Uncles, Cousins)

Name: _____
Address: _____
Phone/Cell: _____
Email: _____
Relationship: _____

Name: _____
Address: _____
Phone/Cell: _____
Email: _____
Relationship: _____

Name: _____
Address: _____
Phone/Cell: _____
Email: _____
Relationship: _____

"ENJOY THE LITTLE THINGS,
FOR ONE DAY YOU MAY LOOK
BACK AND REALIZE THEY
WERE THE BIG THINGS."

~ Robert Brault ~

PART II

ABOUT ME

In this section, you will find important personal information about ME that provides an inside look at what I like to do with my time, things that bring me enjoyment (as well as things I don't necessarily like), foods, as well as music that are my favorites. This is a side of me that is very important to understand.

A future caregiver may have my name and my diagnosis and know the medications that I take…but these pages will tell them more about ME than they will ever find inside a file full of medical records.

This is important material. Here you will find those "inside" facts about ME that will allow anyone reading this to truly come to understand who I am.

ABOUT ME

I AM . . .
MY PROFILE

My Statistics (As of this date:):

    Height: _____

    Weight: _____

    Birthdate: (DD/MM/YYYY) _____

    Eye Color: _____

    Hair Color: _____

    Clothing Size(s):

    Shirt / Blouse: _____

    Pants: _____

    Skirt / Dress: _____

    Outer Coat: _____

    Shoes: _____

    Hat: _____

    Gloves: _____

    Underwear: _____

    Other: _____

    Preferred Colors to Wear: _____

_____

EVERYTHING ABOUT *ME*

If given a choice, my favorite types of clothing to wear include:

_____

_____

Where I Like To Shop:

    Mall: _____

    Favorite Store: _____

    Dislike Shopping _____

Passport Information:

    Number: _____

    Where Issued: _____

    When Issued: _____

    Expiration Date: _____

ABOUT ME

FAVORITE PRODUCT BRANDS

Depending on my age, my choices of the following items are important and it might be good for you to know my preferences.

I prefer to take: (Check one)

    Shower: _____

    Bath: _____

    Morning: _____

    Night: _____

Toothpaste: _____

Mouthwash: _____

Deodorant: _____

Soap: _____

Shampoo / Conditioner: _____

My Mom's perfume to remember her when she is not with me:
_____

My Dad's aftershave to remember him when he is not with me:
_____

Aromas I Like:
_____

Aromas I Dislike:
_____

EVERYTHING ABOUT *ME*

Name of Hair Stylist: _____

Phone: _____

Address: _____

Products I am allergic to:

1. _____
2. _____
3. _____

Bedtime clothing I am most comfortable wearing:

- Pajamas _____
- Underwear _____
- Warm-ups _____
- Other _____

My favorite bed pillow (Check One):

- Soft _____
- Medium _____
- Hard _____
- Other _____

ABOUT ME

Clothes during the day I am most comfortable in:

_____

_____

_____

Fabrics that irritate my skin:

   1. _____

   2. _____

   3. _____

   4. None

The following comments are important about my personal care:

_____

_____

_____

_____

_____

_____

_____

_____

_____

_____

_____

ABOUT ME

I WANT YOU TO KNOW MY PERSONALITY

The following is a description of what it is like to live with me and is written by members of my family.

EVERYTHING ABOUT *ME*

In my own words if possible:

How I would describe myself, my personality traits and characteristics.

_____
_____
_____

What I see as my "abilities" and "skills."

_____
_____
_____

What I see as my "strengths." Example: Will to Live

_____
_____
_____

If appropriate here are descriptions of my "physical abilities."

_____
_____
_____

My "communication skills" can be described as follows:

_____
_____
_____

ABOUT ME

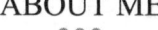

How do I get around?

My sight can be described as:

My hearing is:

Other Abilities:

EVERYTHING ABOUT *ME*

MY TYPICAL DAY

It is important for any caregiver to understand what "I" consider to be a typical day. It is very important that you know how important it is that the routine activities and rituals I enjoy and/or require be maintained as much as possible.

MORNINGS

- If left to my own choice, I am an____early riser or a____late riser (like to sleep in). (Check proper response.)

- I usually wake at_____AM.

- My favorite breakfast consists of:
  _____
  _____
  _____

- My morning usually consists of the following activities (detail everything in a typical morning regimen including exercises, workouts, medications):
  _____
  _____
  _____
  _____

ABOUT ME

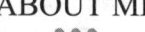

- My favorite fun activities include:

- Activities I dislike:

- Before noon (most days), I have done the following:

- The thing(s) I dislike doing include:

- Things that upset me are:

- How my loved ones handle me when I am upset:

EVERYTHING ABOUT *ME*

- Habits that need improvement (biting my nails, etc.)

_____
_____
_____

AFTERNOONS

- Following lunch, my afternoons usually consist of the following activities (detail everything in a typical afternoon regimen including exercises, workouts, medications):

_____
_____
_____
_____

EVENINGS

- After dinner, the following activities are routine for me (again detail any exercises, workouts, medications and other things considered part of a routine):

_____
_____
_____
_____
_____

- Things I enjoy doing before going to sleep:

_____
_____

- The time I usually like to go to bed: _____

ABOUT ME

MY FAVORITE FOODS

If I'm allowed to make the choices, here they are:

For Breakfast:

_____
_____
_____
_____
_____

For Lunch:

_____
_____
_____
_____
_____

For Dinner:

_____
_____
_____
_____
_____

EVERYTHING ABOUT *ME*

FOOD RESTRICTIONS

ABOUT ME

FOOD FACTS AND ME

I would have these foods around at all times:

_____
_____
_____
_____

List of foods that I truly dislike and will never eat:

_____
_____
_____
_____

Foods I am allergic to:

_____
_____
_____
_____

Eating and drinking capabilities:

Can swallow cold beverages	_____ Yes	_____ No
Can swallow hot beverages	_____ Yes	_____ No
Can chew and swallow cold food	_____ Yes	_____ No
Can chew and swallow hot food	_____ Yes	_____ No
Can use utensils	_____ Yes	_____ No
Can cut food into pieces to chew	_____ Yes	_____ No
Must be fed	_____ Yes	_____ No

EVERYTHING ABOUT *ME*

My favorites:

Candy: _____

Cake: _____

Pie: _____

Ice Cream: _____

Fast Foods: _____

Soups: _____

Salads/Salad
Dressings: _____

Entrees: _____

Cheese: _____

Beverages: _____

Snacks: _____

ABOUT ME

Recipes for food I always enjoy eating:

ABOUT ME

MY PHYSICAL CAPABILITIES

The following describes what I am able to / or not accomplish by myself:

Independence:

Can be left alone

Daytime	_____ Yes	_____ No
Evening	_____ Yes	_____ No

I enjoy being left alone _____ Yes _____ No

Understands concept of "Emergency"

Can respond / react to emergency situations	_____ Yes	_____ No
Can dial 911	_____ Yes	_____ No
Can communicate "Emergency" to police/fire/hospital	_____ Yes	_____ No

Can brush teeth	_____ Yes	_____ No
Can wash own hair	_____ Yes	_____ No
Can brush or comb hair	_____ Yes	_____ No
Can enter bathtub or shower without assistance	_____ Yes	_____ No
Can turn faucets "on" and "off"	_____ Yes	_____ No
Can adjust faucets to "warmer" and "cooler"	_____ Yes	_____ No

EVERYTHING ABOUT *ME*

Can wash self	_____ Yes	_____ No
Can dry self	_____ Yes	_____ No
Can get to and use toilet myself	_____ Yes	_____ No
Can move quickly enough to get to bathroom	_____ Yes	_____ No
Need to be reminded to watch bowels _____	Yes	_____ No
Can shave self	_____ Yes	_____ No
Can select appropriate seasonal clothing	_____ Yes	_____ No
Can dress myself	_____ Yes	_____ No
Can button clothing	_____ Yes	_____ No
Can utilize zippers	_____ Yes	_____ No

Around the house, I can / cannot participate the following:

Can carry laundry	_____ Yes	_____ No
Can sort clothing for the laundry	_____ Yes	_____ No
Can load washer / dryer	_____ Yes	_____ No
Can unload washer / dryer	_____ Yes	_____ No
Can place laundry in drawers	_____ Yes	_____ No
Can place laundry on hangers	_____ Yes	_____ No
Can open plastic food containers	_____ Yes	_____ No
Can use can opener	_____ Yes	_____ No
Can use toaster / toaster oven	_____ Yes	_____ No
Can use microwave	_____ Yes	_____ No

ABOUT ME

Can use stove / oven	_____ Yes	_____ No	
Can remove items from refrigerator	_____ Yes	_____ No	
Can clear dining table	_____ Yes	_____ No	
Can serve food to dining table	_____ Yes	_____ No	
Can rinse dishes	_____ Yes	_____ No	
Can fill / empty dishwasher	_____ Yes	_____ No	
Can use vacuum cleaner	_____ Yes	_____ No	
Can sweep floor with broom	_____ Yes	_____ No	
Can use wet mop	_____ Yes	_____ No	
Can dust	_____ Yes	_____ No	
Can clean toilets	_____ Yes	_____ No	
Can clean bathtubs / showers / sinks	_____ Yes	_____ No	
Can make my bed	_____ Yes	_____ No	

Communications:

Can make use of traditional phone	_____ Yes	_____ No
Can utilize cell phone	_____ Yes	_____ No
Can answer phone / take messages	_____ Yes	_____ No
Can speak comfortably on phone	_____ Yes	_____ No
Can dial "911"	_____ Yes	_____ No
Can communicate "Emergency"	_____ Yes	_____ No

EVERYTHING ABOUT *ME*

Money Making:

Can sort coins by value	_____ Yes	_____ No
Can sort paper currency by value	_____ Yes	_____ No
Gets allowance	_____ Yes	_____ No
Understands "saving"	_____ Yes	_____ No

ABOUT ME

MY FAVORITE ACTIVITIES, HOBBIES PERSONAL INTERESTS & PREFERENCES

If my schedule permits, here is as list (and details of the activities that I enjoy. Those I enjoy most are checkmarked.)

My five top hobbies:

1. _____
2. _____
3. _____
4. _____
5. _____

Reading / Being Read To: (provide details of favorite stories, poems, books)

_____
_____
_____
_____

Games: (Board games, physical games, etc.)

_____
_____
_____
_____

EVERYTHING ABOUT *ME*

Music (Listening & Making) Provide titles of songs / instruments

_____

_____

_____

_____

Singing Ability / Interests:

_____

_____

_____

_____

Art: (Type of activities - drawing, pasting, cutting, molding)

_____

_____

_____

_____

Video Games (Provide Names)

_____

_____

_____

_____

ABOUT ME

Sports (watching, participating) Name specific activities

_____

_____

_____

_____

_____

Other Interests / Talents / Skills

_____

_____

_____

_____

_____

EVERYTHING ABOUT *ME*

ENTERTAINMENT PREFERENCES

My favorite TV show is:

___

My least favorite TV show is:

___

My very favorite movie / cartoon is:

___

My least favorite movie / cartoon is:

___

My favorite music to listen to includes:

___

Type of musical performance I enjoy watching:

Rock concert:

Symphony:

Grand Ole Opry:

Jazz:

Rap / Hip Hop:

Other:

ABOUT ME

My favorite newspaper comic characters / comic books are:

___

___

If I were to pick my favorite book is and why:

___

___

___

___

My favorite authors include:

___

___

Favorite Sports Figures:

___

___

___

___

___

___

Favorite TV Stars:

___

___

___

___

EVERYTHING ABOUT *ME*

CARING FOR MY PETS IN A TIME OF EMERGENCY

PET #1

Type of pet: _____

Name of pet: _____

Pet named _____, does NOT like the following (thought it important to let you know): _____

_____

Specific Health Issues: _____

_____

_____

Medications: _____

_____

Location of Vaccination Information: _____

_____

 **Suggestion:** Consider placing your cell phone number on your pet's collar or consider having a microchip implanted.

ABOUT ME

Veterinarian: Name: _____
                              Phone: _____
                              Address: _____
                                         _____

Pet Groomer: Name: _____
                              Phone: _____
                              Address: _____
                                         _____

Kennel: Name: _____
                              Phone: _____
                              Address: _____
                                         _____

Name / phone number of individual who could care for pet temporarily:

                              Name: _____
                              Phone: _____
                              Address: _____
                                         _____

Brand of General Pet Food:

                              Dry: _____

                              Wet: _____

Brand of Biscuits: _____

Brand of Special Treats: _____

EVERYTHING ABOUT *ME*

Exercise / activity with pet: _____

_____

_____

Where he/she prefers to sleep: _____

_____

_____

Would you like your pet to visit you if possible?

_____ Yes   _____ No

Arrangements for permanent care for my pet – to assure that my pet is loved and properly cared for:

_____

_____

_____

_____

_____

_____

_____

_____

_____

_____

ABOUT ME

CARING FOR MY PETS IN A TIME OF EMERGENCY

PET #2

Type of pet: _____

Name of pet: _____

Pet named _____, does NOT like the following (thought it important to let you know): _____
_____

Specific Health Issues: _____
_____
_____

Medications: _____
_____

Location of Vaccination Information: _____
_____

 **Suggestion:** Affordable health insurance for pets is becoming acceptable among serious pet owners. You can get a list of providers from your local pet shop or by searching the Internet.

EVERYTHING ABOUT *ME*

Veterinarian: Name: _____
              Phone: _____
              Address: _____
              _____

Pet Groomer: Name: _____
              Phone: _____
              Address: _____
              _____

Kennel: Name: _____
              Phone: _____
              Address: _____
              _____

Name / phone number of individual who could care for pet temporarily:

              Name: _____
              Phone: _____
              Address: _____
              _____

Brand of General Pet Food:

              Dry: _____

              Wet: _____

Brand of Biscuits: _____

Brand of Special Treats: _____

ABOUT ME

Exercise / activity with pet: _____
_____
_____

Where he/she prefers to sleep: _____
_____
_____

Would you like your pet to visit you if possible?

_____ Yes   _____ No

Arrangements for permanent care for my pet – to assure that my pet is loved and properly cared for:

_____
_____
_____
_____
_____
_____
_____
_____
_____
_____
_____
_____

EVERYTHING ABOUT *ME*

CARING FOR MY PETS IN A TIME OF EMERGENCY

PET #3

Type of pet: _____

Name of pet: _____

Pet named _____, does NOT like the following
(thought it important to let you know): _____

_____

Specific Health Issues: _____

_____

_____

Medications: _____

_____

Location of Vaccination Information: _____

_____

 **Suggestion:** Any papers/proof that pets have current vaccinations should be kept in a folder/large envelope and clearly marked.

ABOUT ME

Veterinarian: Name: _____
                 Phone: _____
                 Address: _____
                 _____

Pet Groomer: Name: _____
                 Phone: _____
                 Address: _____
                 _____

Kennel: Name: _____
                 Phone: _____
                 Address: _____
                 _____

Name / phone number of individual who could care for pet temporarily:

                 Name: _____
                 Phone: _____
                 Address: _____
                 _____

Brand of General Pet Food:

                 Dry: _____

                 Wet: _____

Brand of Biscuits: _____

Brand of Special Treats: _____

EVERYTHING ABOUT *ME*

Exercise / activity with pet: _____

_____

_____

Where he/she prefers to sleep: _____

_____

_____

Would you like your pet to visit you if possible?

_____ Yes   _____ No

Arrangements for permanent care for my pet – to assure that my pet is loved and properly cared for:

_____

_____

_____

_____

_____

_____

_____

_____

_____

_____

_____

ABOUT ME

ADDITIONAL THINGS I WANT YOU TO KNOW ABOUT ME

MY FAVORITE PEOPLE

If I could have the following people visit with me, come to play, or read to me, here are my favorites:

Name: _____

Age: _____

Relationship: _____

Favorite Thing to Do with Them: _____

Phone #: _____

Email Address: _____

Where They Live: _____

Name: _____

Age: _____

Relationship: _____

Favorite Thing to Do with Them: _____

Phone #: _____

Email Address: _____

Where They Live: _____

EVERYTHING ABOUT *ME*

Name: _____

Age: _____

Relationship: _____

Favorite Thing to Do with Them: _____

_____

Phone #: _____

Email Address: _____

Where They Live: _____

Name: _____

Age: _____

Relationship: _____

Favorite Thing to Do with Them: _____

_____

Phone #: _____

Email Address: _____

Where They Live: _____

ABOUT ME

Things you should know to even further understand me as a person:

If I could do one thing differently in my life, I would . . .

_____
_____
_____

I was so excited when . . .

_____
_____
_____

My favorite part of being in school is . . .

_____
_____
_____

If I could wish for one thing right now, it would be . . .

_____
_____
_____

My favorite place is . . .

_____
_____
_____

What I like most about myself is . . .

_____
_____
_____

EVERYTHING ABOUT *ME*

The most important things I own are . . .

_____

_____

_____

I feel better when I . . .

_____

_____

_____

My greatest fear is . . .

_____

_____

_____

I get upset when . . .

_____

_____

_____

I like to be hugged because . . .

_____

_____

_____

**"TELL ME AND I FORGET.
TEACH ME AND I REMEMBER.
INVOLVE ME AND I LEARN."**

~ Benjamin Franklin ~

ABOUT ME

MY EDUCATION

The following describes my education, in whatever form it is currently or has taken to date. (Complete the sections that apply, depending upon my age and health requirements.)

Few will argue that in the life of an individual with special needs, there are no more important people than parents and teachers. Education, be it within a facility or in a home setting, is an ongoing and critical part of the life of a child with special needs.

If applicable, feel free to check those that apply and make comments to help better understand the current situation. Ignore those areas that don't apply.

Subjects: I enjoy the following subjects (Check any that apply)

_____	Spelling		Science
_____	English	_____	Biology
_____	Reading	_____	Physics
	Social Studies:	_____	Geology
_____	History	_____	Astronomy
_____	Geography	_____	General Science
_____	Philosophy	_____	Math
_____	Economics	_____	Other

EVERYTHING ABOUT *ME*

I am currently attending the following school:

Name: _____

Address: _____

Important Information About the School:

Principal's Name: _____

Guidance Counselor's Name: _____

Teacher's Name: _____

Special Requirements for Me to Attend School:

Name of Transportation Co. _____

Phone #: _____

Bus Driver's Name: _____

For Older Child:

Elementary School Attended: _____

Next School Attended: _____

Next School Attended: _____

See above for current school

ABOUT ME

Readiness School Checklist:

The following may be a guide, if age and health appropriate, for allowing future caregivers to further understand your special individual.

_____ Has been given all school-required immunizations

_____ Gets sufficient rest and is energetic during day

_____ Needs specific daily medical and/or healthcare attention

_____ Knows colors and shapes

_____ Can count

_____ Sorts and classifies things

_____ Can write name

_____ Knows and can write home address

_____ Is/Is Not capable of play activity

    _____ Indoor   _____ Outdoor

_____ Participation in activities that provide exercise is/is not advisable

    Large Muscle Development

        _____ Throwing

        _____ Running

        _____ Jumping

    Small Muscle Development

        _____ Eye-Hand Coordination

        _____ Finger-Hand-Arm Coordination

EVERYTHING ABOUT *ME*

_____	Enjoys drawing
_____	Enjoys listening to music
_____	Enjoys making music
_____	Can move sufficiently to dance
_____	Enjoys / appreciates books
_____	Is regularly read to by parent/guardian/others
_____	Books and materials to stimulate imagination are
_____	Demonstrates self-control
_____	Experiences numerous opportunities to communicate
_____	Encouraged to engaged in conversation
_____	Encouraged to ask questions
_____	Enjoys and is eager to learn
_____	Follows simple instructions
_____	Is curious
_____	Enjoys exploring and trying new experiences
_____	Encouraged to solve problems
_____	Encouraged to notice similarities and differences
_____	Works independently on tasks and assignments
_____	Spends time with other students of the same age
_____	Successfully cooperates with others
_____	Takes tasks through to completion
_____	Encouraged to participate in family chores
_____	There is adult supervised television viewing in my home

ABOUT ME

MY EDUCATIONAL SUPPORT TEAM

The following are individuals who mean a great deal to my family, and me when it comes to my education.

Name: _____

Address: _____

Phone: _____

Email: _____

His/Her Special Role: _____

Name: _____

Address: _____

Phone: _____

Email: _____

His/Her Special Role: _____

Name: _____

Address: _____

Phone: _____

Email: _____

His/Her Special Role: _____

EVERYTHING ABOUT *ME*

EMPLOYMENT

Name of Organization: _____

Address: _____

Phone: _____

Email: _____

My Responsibility: _____

Immediate Supervisor: _____

Phone: _____

Benefit Plans: _____
_____
_____

Special Needs to Get To and From Work: (Wheelchair, Transportation, Etc.)
_____
_____
_____
_____

Attitude

The longer I live, the more I realize the impact of attitude on life. Attitude, to me, is more important than facts. It is important than the past, than education, than money, than circumstances, than failures, than successes, than what other people think or say or do. It is more important than appearance, giftedness or skill. It will make or break a company... a church... a home. The remarkable thing is we have a choice every day regarding the attitude we will embrace for that day. We cannot change our past... we cannot change the fact that people will act in a certain way. We cannot change the inevitable. The only thing we can do is play on the one string we have, and that is our attitude. I am convinced that life is 10% what happens to me and 90% how I react to it. And so it is with you... we are in charge of our Attitudes.

~Anonymous ~

MEDICAL

PART III

THE MEDICAL SIDE OF LIFE

Obviously, knowing the critical healthcare information about ME will enable caregivers in the future to have a better understanding of where I've been and have experienced.

As the following pages are completed, keep in mind that each section will serve ME best in the future, if every detail is addressed. You may want to use a pencil, since some information will change over time.

* NOTE: Whenever there is a change in medications, attending physicians, therapy treatment, etc., be sure to update the information immediately. Always be consistent, when entering dosage of medications, entries regarding attending healthcare professionals, legal documents, etc.

MEDICAL

WHAT'S IMPORTANT FOR YOU TO KNOW ABOUT ME MEDICALLY

I HAVE A DIAGNOSIS OF: _____

_____

Date of Diagnosis: _____

Age of Occurrence: _____

Facility Diagnosis was Made at: _____

Doctor / Group Making Diagnosis: _____

Records retained by (Doctor / Group): _____

Immediate Supervisor: _____

_____
_____
_____
_____
_____
_____

Note: Four diagnosis pages are provided in this section. If more information is needed, place in note section.

EVERYTHING ABOUT *ME*

I HAVE A DIAGNOSIS OF: _____

_____

Date of Diagnosis: _____

Age of Occurrence: _____

Facility Diagnosis was Made at: _____

Doctor / Group Making Diagnosis: _____

Records retained by (Doctor / Group): _____

Current Treatment / Regimen: _____

_____
_____
_____
_____
_____
_____
_____
_____
_____
_____
_____
_____
_____

MEDICAL

I HAVE A DIAGNOSIS OF: _____

_____

Date of Diagnosis: _____

Age of Occurrence: _____

Facility Diagnosis was Made at: _____

Doctor / Group Making Diagnosis: _____

Records retained by (Doctor / Group): _____

Current Treatment / Regimen: _____

EVERYTHING ABOUT *ME*

I HAVE A DIAGNOSIS OF: _____

_____

Date of Diagnosis: _____

Age of Occurrence: _____

Facility Diagnosis was Made at: _____

Doctor / Group Making Diagnosis: _____

Records retained by (Doctor / Group): _____

Current Treatment / Regimen: _____

_____
_____
_____
_____
_____
_____
_____
_____
_____
_____
_____
_____
_____
_____
_____

MEDICAL

MEDICATIONS PRESCRIBED

Drug: _____
Dosage: _____
# of Doses / Day: _____
When Taken: _____ AM / Time _____ Noon _____ PM / Time
Prescribed by (Physician): _____
Condition Prescribed For: _____

Drug: _____
Dosage: _____
# of Doses / Day: _____
When Taken: _____ AM / Time _____ Noon _____ PM / Time
Prescribed by (Physician): _____
Condition Prescribed For: _____

Drug: _____
Dosage: _____
# of Doses / Day: _____
When Taken: _____ AM / Time _____ Noon _____ PM / Time
Prescribed by (Physician): _____
Condition Prescribed For: _____

Drug: _____
Dosage: _____
# of Doses / Day: _____
When Taken: _____ AM / Time _____ Noon _____ PM / Time
Prescribed by (Physician): _____
Condition Prescribed For: _____

EVERYTHING ABOUT *ME*

Drug: _____
Dosage: _____
# of Doses / Day: _____
When Taken: _____ AM / Time _____ Noon _____ PM / Time
Prescribed by (Physician): _____
Condition Prescribed For: _____

Drug: _____
Dosage: _____
# of Doses / Day: _____
When Taken: _____ AM / Time _____ Noon _____ PM / Time
Prescribed by (Physician): _____
Condition Prescribed For: _____

Drug: _____
Dosage: _____
# of Doses / Day: _____
When Taken: _____ AM / Time _____ Noon _____ PM / Time
Prescribed by (Physician): _____
Condition Prescribed For: _____

Drug: _____
Dosage: _____
# of Doses / Day: _____
When Taken: _____ AM / Time _____ Noon _____ PM / Time
Prescribed by (Physician): _____
Condition Prescribed For: _____

MEDICAL

ACROSS-THE-COUNTER DRUGS - PHARMACEUTICAL & HOMEOPATHIC

Drug: _____

Dosage: _____

# of Doses / Day: _____

When Taken: _____ AM / Time _____ Noon _____ PM / Time

Condition Prescribed For: _____

Drug: _____

Dosage: _____

# of Doses / Day: _____

When Taken: _____ AM / Time _____ Noon _____ PM / Time

Condition Prescribed For: _____

Drug: _____

Dosage: _____

# of Doses / Day: _____

When Taken: _____ AM / Time _____ Noon _____ PM / Time

Condition Prescribed For: _____

Drug: _____

Dosage: _____

# of Doses / Day: _____

When Taken: _____ AM / Time _____ Noon _____ PM / Time

Condition Prescribed For: _____

EVERYTHING ABOUT *ME*

Drug: _____

Dosage: _____

# of Doses / Day: _____

When Taken: _____ AM / Time _____ Noon _____ PM / Time

Condition Prescribed For: _____

Drug: _____

Dosage: _____

# of Doses / Day: _____

When Taken: _____ AM / Time _____ Noon _____ PM / Time

Condition Prescribed For: _____

Drug: _____

Dosage: _____

# of Doses / Day: _____

When Taken: _____ AM / Time _____ Noon _____ PM / Time

Condition Prescribed For: _____

Drug: _____

Dosage: _____

# of Doses / Day: _____

When Taken: _____ AM / Time _____ Noon _____ PM / Time

Condition Prescribed For: _____

Drug: _____

Dosage: _____

# of Doses / Day: _____

When Taken: _____ AM / Time _____ Noon _____ PM / Time

Condition Prescribed For: _____

MEDICAL

IMMUNIZATION INFORMATION

Vaccine	Type	Date Administered	Doctor Source

EVERYTHING ABOUT *ME*

DRUG & MEDICAL ALLERGIES

I am allergic to the following (check):

_____ Foods (nuts, shellfish, dairy, etc. - list):
_____
_____

_____	Latex	_____	Epenephrin
_____	Iodine	_____	Insulin
_____	Adhesive Tape	_____	Bee Stings
_____	Aspirin	_____	Pollin
_____	Penicillin	_____	Histamines
_____	Corticosteroids	_____	Dander
_____	Immunoglobulins		

_____ Antibiotics (list)
_____

_____ Plants (list)
_____

_____ Other (list)
_____

MEDICAL

MY MEDICAL / HEALTHCARE SUPPORT TEAM

PRIMARY PHYSICIAN:

Name: _____

Address: _____

Phone: _____

Cell Phone: _____

SPECIALTY PHYSICIANS:

Name: _____

Address: _____

Phone: _____

Cell Phone: _____

Specialty / Frequency of Visits: _____

_____

Name: _____

Address: _____

Phone: _____

Cell Phone: _____

Specialty / Frequency of Visits: _____

EVERYTHING ABOUT *ME*

SPECIALTY PHYSICIANS - cont:

Name: _____

Address: _____

Phone: _____

Cell Phone:

Specialty / Frequency of Visits: _____

_____

Name: _____

Address: _____

Phone: _____

Cell Phone:

Specialty / Frequency of Visits: _____

_____

I am "anxious" when I must go to the doctor's office:

_____ Yes   _____ No

What is done to calm me down:

_____

_____

Hospital I prefer in case of illness or accident:

Name: _____

Address: _____

Phone: _____

MEDICAL

IMPORTANT PEOPLE WHO ARE MY HELPERS

Personal caregiver, aide:

Name: _____

Address: _____

Phone: _____

Email: _____

His/Her Special Role: _____

Personal representative:

Name: _____

Address: _____

Phone: _____

Email: _____

His/Her Special Role: _____

Trustee:

Name: _____

Address: _____

Phone: _____

Email: _____

His/Her Special Role: _____

EVERYTHING ABOUT *ME*

Dentist:

Name: _____

Address: _____

Phone: _____

Optometrist:

Name: _____

Address: _____

Phone: _____

Optician:

Name: _____

Address: _____

Phone: _____

Other (Specify):

Name: _____

Address: _____

Phone: _____

Other (Specify):

Name: _____

Address: _____

Phone: _____

MEDICAL

PROGRAMS THAT I PARTICIPATE IN REGULARLY

Name of Program: _____

Location: _____

_____

Primary Contact:

Name: _____

Phone: _____

Schedule: _____

Activities / Therapies / Treatments: _____

_____

_____

Name of Program: _____

Location: _____

_____

Primary Contact:

Name: _____

Phone: _____

Schedule: _____

Activities / Therapies / Treatments: _____

_____

_____

EVERYTHING ABOUT *ME*

Name of Program: _____

Location: _____

_____

Primary Contact:

Name: _____

Phone: _____

Schedule: _____

Activities / Therapies / Treatments: _____

_____

_____

Name of Program: _____

Location: _____

_____

Primary Contact:

Name: _____

Phone: _____

Schedule: _____

Activities / Therapies / Treatments: _____

_____

_____

FAMILY MEDICAL HISTORY

Family medical history remains the best genetic tool we have.

- Maternal range of health conditions:

_____
_____
_____
_____
_____
_____
_____
_____
_____
_____

- Paternal range of health conditions:

_____
_____
_____
_____
_____
_____
_____
_____
_____
_____

> **"ONE NEVER NOTICES WHAT HAS BEEN DONE; ONE CAN ONLY SEE WHAT REMAINS TO BE DONE."**
>
> *~ Marie Curie ~*

FINANCES

PART IV

FINANCIALLY CARING FOR ME

The following may be part of the plan for caring for my needs each month. Check those that apply (and make comments where necessary).

EVERYTHING ABOUT *ME*

INCOME SOURCES

Government Benefits: (Explain)

_____
_____
_____
_____
_____

Gifts / Support from Family / Relatives : (Explain)

_____
_____
_____
_____
_____
_____

Other Sources: (Explain)

_____
_____
_____
_____
_____

FINANCES

DETAILS OF MY PERSONAL MONTHLY EXPENSES

- Only your family knows the true nature of your expenses.
- Please use all items that apply.

Housing: My % of family expenses:	$ Total	Contact Phone #
Mortgage or Rent		
Utilities		
Gas		
Water		
Electric		
Telephone		
Cable		
Cleaning		
Laundry		
House		
Property		
Maintenance		
Other		
Total		

*This section may not include all expenses your family / guardians experience each month. Please expand as needed.

EVERYTHING ABOUT *ME*

Equipment:

	$ Total	Contact Phone #
Wheelchair		
Computer		
Life System		
Automatic Bed		
Elevator		
Guide Dog		
Hearing Aid		
Maintenance		
Other		
Total		

Personal Care:

	$ Total	Contact Phone #
Live-in Aides		
Custodial Care		
Respite for Caregivers		
Other		
Total		

FINANCES

Personal Needs:

	$ Total	Contact Phone #
Grooming		
Haircuts		
Other		
Other		
Other		
Total		

Education:

	$ Total	Contact Phone #
Homebound		
Tutors		
Books		
Supplies		
Transportation		
Other		
Total		

Transportation:

	$ Total	Contact Phone #
Family Vehicle		
Tutors		
Upkeep		
Other		
Total		

EVERYTHING ABOUT *ME*

My Pet(s):

	$ Total	Contact Phone #
Food		
Vet		
Training		
Other		
Total		

Social Activities:

	$ Total	Contact Phone #
Vacation(s)		
Special Needs		
Special Olympics		
Equipment Rentals		
Events		
Other		
Total		

Additional / Misc. Expenses

List	$ Total	Contact Phone #
Total		

"THE NICE THING ABOUT TEAMWORK IS THAT YOU ALWAYS HAVE OTHERS ON YOUR SIDE."

~ Margaret Carty ~

PART V

MY NON-MEDICAL PLANNING TEAM

The following is a grouping of people / groups the play an important part in my life and that of my family. They are outside the direct "medical-healthcare" arena, but just as important.

NON-MEDICAL PLANNING TEAM

Attorney:
Name: _____
Phone: _____
Address: _____
Email: _____
Specialty _____

Accountant:
Name: _____
Phone: _____
Address: _____
Email: _____
Specialty _____

Financial Planner:
Name: _____
Phone: _____
Address: _____
Email: _____
Specialty _____

Insurance Provider:
Name: _____
Phone: _____
Address: _____
Email: _____
Specialty _____

NON-MEDICAL PLANNING TEAM

INSURANCE POLICIES

Should any life insurance policies exist with me as the insured, the following information may one day prove important.

Life Insurance:

Name of Insurance Company _____

Insurance Company Phone # _____

Policy # _____

Group # _____

Member ID # (If Applicable) _____

Co-pays # (If Applicable) _____

Address of Company _____

_____

Location of Policy _____

Life Insurance:

Name of Insurance Company _____

Insurance Company Phone # _____

Policy # _____

Group # _____

Member ID # (If Applicable) _____

Co-pays # (If Applicable) _____

Address of Company _____

_____

Location of Policy _____

EVERYTHING ABOUT *ME*

ADDITIONAL INSURANCE:

If any additional forms of insurance covers ME, here is the appropriate information:

Health Insurance:

Name of Insurance Company _____

Insurance Company Phone # _____

Policy # _____

Group # _____

Member ID # (If Applicable) _____

Co-pays # (If Applicable) _____

Address of Company _____

Location of Policy _____

Long-Term Health Insurance:

Name of Insurance Company _____

Insurance Company Phone # _____

Policy # _____

Group # _____

Member ID # (If Applicable) _____

Co-pays # (If Applicable) _____

Address of Company _____

Location of Policy _____

NON-MEDICAL PLANNING TEAM

Dental Insurance:

Name of Insurance Company _____
Insurance Company Phone # _____
Policy # _____
Group # _____
Member ID # (If Applicable) _____
Co-pays # (If Applicable) _____
Address of Company _____
Location of Policy _____

Vision Insurance:

Name of Insurance Company _____
Insurance Company Phone # _____
Policy # _____
Group # _____
Member ID # (If Applicable) _____
Co-pays # (If Applicable) _____
Address of Company _____
Location of Policy _____

Other Insurance:

Name of Insurance Company _____
Insurance Company Phone # _____
Policy # _____
Group # _____
Member ID # (If Applicable) _____
Co-pays # (If Applicable) _____
Address of Company _____
Location of Policy _____

ESTATE & LEGAL PLANNING

Locating and understanding where important papers can be found (provide location, contact person if needed, contact phone numbers):

Estate and Legal

Location: _____

_____
_____
_____

Specific notes and comments on estate and legal planning:

_____
_____
_____
_____
_____
_____
_____
_____
_____
_____
_____
_____
_____

NON-MEDICAL PLANNING TEAM

POWER OF ATTORNEY

Two people with LEGAL Powers of Attorney:

Name: _____

Address: _____

_____

_____

Cell #: _____

Phone #: _____

Name: _____

Address: _____

_____

_____

Cell #: _____

Phone #: _____

Comments: _____

_____

_____

_____

EVERYTHING ABOUT *ME*

POWER OF ATTORNEY

Two people with HEALTHCARE Powers of Attorney:

Name: _____

Address: _____
_____

Cell #: _____

Phone #: _____

Name: _____

Address: _____
_____

Cell #: _____

Phone #: _____

Comments: _____
_____
_____

NON-MEDICAL PLANNING TEAM

BIRTH CERTIFICATE & PASSPORT

BIRTH CERTIFICATE:

Two people with copies of my birth certificate:

Name: _____

Address: _____

_____

_____

Cell #: _____

Phone #: _____

Name: _____

Address: _____

_____

_____

Cell #: _____

Phone #: _____

PASSPORT:

Location: _____

ID: _____

Where Issued: _____

Date Issued: _____

Expiration Date: _____

EVERYTHING ABOUT *ME*

MY FAMILY'S SOCIAL SUPPORT TEAM

The following are people who have taken a personal interest in the well-being of my parents/guardians and me, who make themselves available at all hours of the day and night when called upon.

Name: _____ Affiliation: _____

Address: _____

Phone: _____

Email: _____

His/Her Special Role: _____

Name: _____ Affiliation: _____

Address: _____

Phone: _____

Email: _____

His/Her Special Role: _____

Name: _____ Affiliation: _____

Address: _____

Phone: _____

Email: _____

His/Her Special Role: _____

NON-MEDICAL PLANNING TEAM

LOCAL, STATE & FEDERAL GOVERNMENT ASSISTANCE

Name of Department: _____
Address: _____
Phone: _____
Contact Person: _____
Email: _____
Services / Notes _____
_____

Name of Department: _____
Address: _____
Phone: _____
Contact Person: _____
Email: _____
Services / Notes _____
_____

Name of Department: _____
Address: _____
Phone: _____
Contact Person: _____
Email: _____
Services / Notes _____
_____

EVERYTHING ABOUT *ME*

Name of Organization: _____

Address: _____

Phone: _____

Contact Person: _____

Email: _____

Specialty Services / Notes _____

_____

Name of Organization: _____

Address: _____

Phone: _____

Contact Person: _____

Email: _____

Specialty Services / Notes _____

_____

Name of Organization: _____

Address: _____

Phone: _____

Contact Person: _____

Email: _____

Specialty Services / Notes _____

_____

NON-MEDICAL PLANNING TEAM

MY PERSONAL & FAMILY ADVOCACY SUPPORT TEAM

The following organizations with whom my parents / guardians have minimal to very close contact.

Name of Organization: _____
Address: _____
Phone: _____
Contact Person: _____
Email: _____
Specialty Services / Notes _____
_____

Name of Organization: _____
Address: _____
Phone: _____
Contact Person: _____
Email: _____
Specialty Services / Notes _____
_____

Name of Organization: _____
Address: _____
Phone: _____
Contact Person: _____
Email: _____
Specialty Services / Notes _____
_____

"I AM NOT AFRAID OF TOMORROW, FOR I HAVE SEEN YESTERDAY AND I LOVE TODAY."

~ William Allen White ~

MY FUTURE CARE

PART VI

MY FUTURE CARE

> Should my parents/guardians precede me in death, the following pages will provide additional information on how they "saw" my future. It is important that the information that follows be respected.
>
> When making decisions about my future care, please take the following into consideration, because this is very important and reflect the wishes of me and my parents/guardians.

EVERYTHING ABOUT *ME*

CAREGIVING

The following is a list of preferred caregiving issues that are important to my parents/guardians.

If we _____ (Name of parents/ guardians die before _____ (Name of special person), we desire to have the following person(s) take over the guardianship and maintain future caregiving.

Name: _____
Relationship: _____
Address: _____
Phone: _____
Email: _____
Location of Guardianship Papers: _____

Name: _____
Relationship: _____
Address: _____
Phone: _____
Email: _____
Location of Guardianship Papers: _____

Name: _____
Relationship: _____
Address: _____
Phone: _____
Email: _____
Location of Guardianship Papers: _____

Signed: _____ (Name)

Signed: _____ (Name)

MY FUTURE CARE

IF AND WHEN I FACE A TERMINAL SITUATION

MY parents/guardians will decide at what age (level of maturity) I will be told that my challenges are terminal. They will decide how to share this information with me.

Here is what I have been told and understand about my situation:

EVERYTHING ABOUT *ME*

There are important decisions that may have to be made regarding my care in the future. Perhaps I will be capable of being involved in the decision-making. Here are some issues that may be addressed:

Is there a Living Will:

_____ Yes

_____ No

Location: _____

Who holds copies: _____

Is there a Healthcare Directive

_____ Yes

_____ No

Location: _____

Who holds copies: _____

My parents/guardians want the following to be done in a medical emergency:

If my heart stops, do_____ do not _____ use CPR (cardiopulmonary resuscitation).

Do _____ Do not_____ place on any mechanical breathing apparatus.

Do _____ Do Not_____ administer blood transfusions.

Do _____ Do Not_____ administer intravenous food administered.

MY FUTURE CARE

ORGAN DONATION

My parents/guardians have decided to permit me (if I am under legal age) to be an organ donor. If I am of legal age, my decision is:

_____   Yes

_____   No

Personal Comments on Organ Donation:
_____
_____
_____
_____

Any Special Requests Regarding Organ Donation:
_____
_____
_____
_____

Location of Official Documentation:
_____
_____
_____
_____

"THERE ARE ONLY TWO WAYS TO LIVE... ONE IS AS THOUGH NOTHING IS A MIRACLE... THE OTHER IS AS IF EVERYTHING IS."

~ Albert Einstein ~

PART VII

FAITH & RELIGION IN MY LIFE

The following may be very important for others in order for them to better understand me. The information here should be age appropriate and may change over time. Please note that my parents/guardians put this information here, so that you will understand the importance of my spiritual life.

EVERYTHING ABOUT *ME*

RELIGIOUS AFFILIATION

Church, Synagogue, Mosque, Temple, Other Religious Facility:
_____

Address: _____

Telephone #: _____

E-mail address: _____

Web site: _____

Key Contact Person(s):

    Name: _____

    Cell Phone: _____

    Name: _____

    Cell Phone: _____

Describe my Involvement / Attendance:
_____
_____
_____

Special requirements needed for me to attend services:
_____
_____
_____

Where I Like to Sit: _____

Time of Day I Prefer to Attend Service: _____

FAITH & RELIGION

My favorite stories, scriptures, songs, hymn:

The importance of my faith in my life:

EVERYTHING ABOUT *ME*

REFLECTIONS ON MY LIFE THUS FAR

In the words of my parents/guardians, here is how they see what can be called "My Philosophy of Life." If possible, in my own words: This is what I'd like to share with those who know me and those who don't, but may in the future.

_____

_____

_____

_____

_____

_____

_____

_____

_____

_____

_____

_____

_____

_____

_____

_____

_____

_____

FAITH & RELIGION

How I'd like (or my parents/guardians would like me) to be remembered:

EVERYTHING ABOUT *ME*

A Letter For My Loved Ones

These are my words, written down/dictated by me, an intended for those in my life that mean so much.

"THE BEST AND MOST BEAUTIFUL THINGS IN THE WORLD CANNOT BE SEEN OR EVEN TOUCHED. THEY MUST BE FELT WITH THE HEART."

~ Helen Keller ~

PART VIII

HOLIDAYS, TRADITIONS & MEMORIES

> **NOTE:** For many people, there are standard holidays that are observed such as Thanksgiving or the 4th of July. However, each family has many holidays to select from in any given year. Depending on one's religious preferences, family structure, and other reasons, you can customize this section to fit your individual preferences (such as Christmas, Hanukkah, Easter, Ramadan, Kwanzaa for example).

EVERYTHING ABOUT *ME*

My favorite holiday:

_____
_____
_____
_____
_____
_____

Why this holidays has always been so special:

_____
_____
_____
_____
_____

How I like to celebrate this holiday:

_____
_____
_____
_____
_____

HOLIDAYS, MEMORIES & TRADITIONS

Holidays my family celebrates:

Holiday

Family Tradition Observed _____

_____
_____
_____
_____
_____
_____

Holiday

Family Tradition Observed _____

_____
_____
_____
_____
_____
_____

Holiday

Family Tradition Observed _____

_____
_____
_____
_____
_____
_____

EVERYTHING ABOUT *ME*

What I love to do on my favorite holiday:

_____
_____
_____
_____
_____
_____

Holiday vacation(s) I have enjoyed the most (such as a visit to the seashore, to the mountains, taking a cruise, etc.):

_____
_____
_____
_____
_____
_____
_____
_____
_____
_____
_____

HOLIDAYS, MEMORIES & TRADITIONS

Family History & Memories

Before my birth, the following events occurred with my family: (Example - my grandfather was in WWII)

EVERYTHING ABOUT *ME*

The person who has most influenced my life (and how):

HOLIDAYS, MEMORIES & TRADITIONS

My Dad's "Memory Box"

Happy memories spent with me:

1.
2.
3.
4.

My Mom's "Memory Box"

Happy memories spent with me:

1.
2.
3.
4.

"EVERY PERSON, ALL THE EVENTS OF YOUR LIFE ARE THERE BECAUSE YOU HAVE DRAWN THEM THERE. WHAT YOU CHOOSE TO DO WITH THEM IS UP TO YOU."

~ Richard Bach ~

MEMORIAL PREFERENCES

PART IX

MEMORIAL PREFERENCES

This section details preferences for memorial services, locations for services, any pre-arrangements, individuals and organizations to be contacted and information to be included in an obituary.

EVERYTHING ABOUT *ME*

PREFERRED FUNERAL ARRANGEMENTS

At my passing, the following plans have been thought out by my parents/guardians (and are subject to change over time).

Funeral Home:
Name: _____
Phone: _____
Address: _____
_____

My parents/guardians prefer:

☐ Buried ☐ Placed in a Mausoleum ☐ Cremated*

Cemetary _____
Address _____
City/State _____
*Disbursement of Ashes: _____

Burial Plot Location _____
Gravesite # _____
Location of Deed _____
Payment Records
for Perpetual Care _____

Pre-arranged funeral plans: _____
_____
_____

MEMORIAL PREFERENCES

My parents/guardians prefer that I be dressed in the following clothing:

_____
_____
_____

These items should be placed in the coffin with me:

_____
_____
_____
_____

This church/temple/place of worship is to be used for the ceremony (name of location, city):

    Location   _____
    City/State   _____

This Priest, Rabbi, or Clergyman should preside over the ceremony:

    Name: _____
    Phone: _____
    Address   _____

EVERYTHING ABOUT *ME*

My parents/guardians prefer the following pallbearers:

Name: _____
Phone: _____
Cell Phone: _____
E-mail address: _____
Address: _____

Name: _____
Phone: _____
Cell Phone: _____
E-mail address: _____
Address: _____

Name: _____
Phone: _____
Cell Phone: _____
E-mail address: _____
Address: _____

Name: _____
Phone: _____
Cell Phone: _____
E-mail address: _____
Address: _____

MEMORIAL PREFERENCES

I would like the following flowers:

_____
_____
_____
_____

In lieu of flowers, I would like:

_____
_____
_____
_____

I would like the following donations made in my memory (list organizations, groups, individuals):

_____
_____
_____
_____

I would like the following music played at the place of worship:

_____
_____
_____

I would like to have the following inscribed on my tombstone or grave marker:

_____
_____
_____

EVERYTHING ABOUT *ME*

I would like the following included in my obituary:

Notes

The following space is provided for individuals to add all of the "extra information" that hasn't been presented in other parts of this guide - or to embellish things said earlier but requiring additional space. Anything goes here. Feel free to give future caregivers more insight into the real you.

EVERYTHING ABOUT *ME*

Notes

Notes

EVERYTHING ABOUT *ME*

Notes

NOTES

Notes

Notes

Notes

EVERYTHING ABOUT *ME*

Notes

Notes

EVERYTHING ABOUT *ME*

Notes

Notes

EVERYTHING ABOUT *ME*

Notes

Notes

Notes

NOTES

Notes

EVERYTHING ABOUT *ME*

Notes

NOTES

Notes

EVERYTHING ABOUT *ME*

Notes

THIS BOOK IS 'LOVE INSURANCE' FOR YOUR FAMILY. THE PREMIUMS ARE LOW, BUT THE DIVIDENDS ARE PRICELESS!

~ Dee Marrella ~

EVERYTHING ABOUT *ME*

AUTHOR'S NOTES

"The opposite of love is not hate, but indifference." You have proven your love and concern by taking the time to fill this book out. By doing so, you have more peace of mind knowing any caregiver has a "tool" – a "roadmap" to follow when caring for your child with special needs. You have done your very best to see that he / she has the best possible care in the future.

I have labeled this book "Love Insurance" – and like the love of a parent – love insurance never expires.

EVERYTHING ABOUT *ME*

ABOUT DEE MARRELLA

Dee Marrella has experienced life as both a military and a corporate wife. As a result, she has seen much of the world and been exposed to many varied cultures. Born in Paterson, New Jersey, Dee spent twenty-plus years in the field of education in both Europe and the United States. She worked with children with special needs during those assignments. Experiencing those different cultures afforded her the opportunity to observe first hand the vast differences in the ways caregivers interact with both young and old individuals within societies. Today she is the proud wife of retired Colonel and businessman, Len Marrella, the mother of three grown daughters, and the grandmother of seven grandchildren.

Dee was a caregiver for six years and knows firsthand how important it is to have knowledge and guidance in order to do the best job possible.

ABOUT DENNIS McCLELLAN

Dennis McClellan, the publisher of DC Press, who resides outside of Orlando, Florida, has been involved in producing books for professionals in healthcare, medicine and the law for nearly forty years.

He is the proud father of three adult children. His first child was born prematurely, with a number of physical challenges that ended his life during his first month. The lack of knowledge on the part of the doctors, at the time, sparked a real interest in children (and their families) facing lives with special needs. Publishing permitted an opportunity to get involved and provide much-needed information for everyone involved, who seek answers.

Dee Marrella's concept of "future caregiving" is so vitally important, that Dennis jumped at the chance to assist in laying out the content and design of this book.

PUBLISHER'S COMMENTS

All the publishers I know, hope and pray for a project to come along that really lights a fire under them and provides their audiences the most engaging experience possible. We all hope for a book that just reaches out and grabs the reader (user) and gives them the most value for the time they invest. The book that you are holding isn't fiction. It doesn't have thrilling chase scenes, nor does it have heroes that overcome evil and save the world. This book is real life and the hero is YOU.

In the society we live in, it is becoming rare to find close-knit families, adult children who live geographically close to their parents and siblings, or a real feeling of community. As we age, such things become more important. And when we think about our own future such as the possibility of being cared for by others, we tend to imagine that we'll be cared for by members of our immediate family (such as a surviving spouse or adult children). This may becoming more of a dream than a reality. Statistics strongly indicate that the majority of us will be cared for by strangers people outside our family people who do not know who we are.

We have found that caring for others is a valuable gift that we an give one that gives meaning to family and friends during the last years (of days) of their lives. We have also found that caring for others gives us a better feeling about ourselves. There really is meaning to giving of oneself and ones' time. However, while we are caring for others, the vast majority of us fail to "think" or "consider that one day, we'll be in need of care. And when that day comes, will we be prepared?

The answer isn't good: "NO." Most Americans do not think about how they will be cared for in the future. Sure, we purchase life insurance. We buy car, home, property, and health insurance. We even insure cell phones and

EVERYTHING ABOUT *ME*

flat screen TV's against damage. We buy into retirement plans and feed investments. We purchase retirement homes. BUT...do we really give consideration to who will be caring for our medical needs, feeding us, cleaning us, spending time reading with us? Most of us don't.

Dee Marrella has created the most engaging means for YOU to "tell" those people in your future "everything about yourself." From birth through school, from the type of jobs you've held to the hobbies you spend your private time working on, Everything About ME provides you an opportunity to write down the key facts the most important bits of data about YOU. Since few of us actually talk with our spouses about such topics (let alone our children), there are few people (if any) who really know anything, in depth, about ourselves.

Consider that one day you might wake up, let's say, from a coma. You don't know your surroundings. The smells are different than you're used to. The TV in the room is on, but it is showing a Clint Eastwood movie and doesn't anyone know that you just hate Clint Eastwood movies? Someone walks by and smiles at you. You don't recognize their face. And, they don't speak to you. They just walk by. As you follow them, you decide to say something ask a question. BUT, to your surprise, you can't speak. You've had a stroke and can't move a part of your body, and your voice is silent.

This is just one example of when "the book" (Everything About ME) comes into play.

If you had completed the pages of this book. If you had discussed your thoughts and comments with your spouse, adult children, other family, and friends (including an attorney and your physician), there would be a number of people who had become educated about who you are and who you were (in your younger days).

EVERYTHING ABOUT *ME*

Dee Marrella has set up a process whereby YOU can answer questions, tell people about your "likes" and "dislikes," let the world in on who you were back in elementary school, the first musical instrument you attempted to play, the kinds of movies you enjoy, foods that really are your favorites and those you just hate. Without this information readily available in one location, in one format, there is little possibility that anyone will completely know who you are. AND, if you can't speak and tell them, how will they find out?

Rather than becoming a name, an account number, a person with ten medications to take each day, and little else, wouldn't you prefer that those who care for you in the future know who you are? Wouldn't you want to have a voice in your future care? Wouldn't you want people to know how you feel about important issues, such as: life support, organ transplants, healthcare professionals that you prefer take care of you, and how you'd like your funeral to be handled?

All of this can now be under your control. YOU have a copy of one of the most important books published. And when you've completed filling out the pages, you will have a gift for your future caregivers that no one else could have produced. You are the only one. You have the answers. Aren't you glad that you've taken the time to share yourself with the future? Those who care for you will be very pleased.

Your journey is about t begin. Enjoy the trip. And…one day, appreciate the results. YOU are doing a great thing for yourself.

Dennis McClellan, Publisher
DC Press

EVERYTHING ABOUT *ME*

If you found this book thought provoking and would like to have Dee Marrella speak to your organization, please feel free to contact her at:

Dee Marrella

Phone: 610.478.3000
Fax: 610.478.3001
dee@deemarrella.com
www.deemarrella.com

PRESS LLC
www.focusonethics.com
www.dcpressbooks.com

EVERYTHING ABOUT *ME*

Copy, cut and carry this information in your wallet. In case of accident or emergency, it will provide important information about your special need child.

**This Card Contains Information About
My Child with Special Needs**

In Case of Emergency Provide Medical Treatment And Care,
Including Food And Water)

His/Her Name: _____

Please contact:

Name: _____

Phone: _____

Cell: _____

Name: _____

Phone: _____

Cell: _____

Please Print All Information Legibly - See Back For More
_____

Child's Blood Type: _____

Medications:_____
_____

Is allergic to: _____
_____

Is diabetic: _____

Wears contacts: _____

Has Asthma: _____

Is hearing impaired: _____

Is visually impaired: _____

Other conditions: _____
_____

◀ Fold Here ▶